WHEN LIFE MEETS THE SOUL

Bible Study Guide

Ivan D. Parke and Timothy J. Peabody

A 10-week, small-group Bible study on Job
To accompany the book
When Life Meets the Soul: Everyday Lessons from the Book of Job
by Ivan D. Parke

When Life Meets the Soul Bible Study Guide

Print design: Kent Mummert

Cover image: Porthcawl Lighthouse, South Wales, UK. Photograph by Leighton Collins, Adobe Stock 177561850

ISBN: 979-8-3676-0525-9

Table of Contents

Introduction

Each of us experiences tragedy. Nothing, including our relationship with God, makes us exempt from pain and suffering.

When tragedy strikes, we are often careful to make this comforting distinction: God may have *allowed* this evil, but he did not cause it. However, when Satan struck Job's household with tragedy, Job made no such distinction. In fact, Job declared God was the cause of his disaster.

Immediately afterwards, he worshiped, declaring, "The Lord has taken away" (Job 1:21). What Job said reflected his wordview: God is the cause, not God is the culprit (WLMTS, p. 21).

Job believed God was the *cause* of his suffering, but he did not believe God was the *culprit*. Job believed God was the cause of his suffering, but that did not prevent him from worshiping. "The Lord gave, and the Lord has taken away; blessed be the name of the Lord," Job said (Job 1:21).

What was the narrator's response to Job's belief that the Lord had taken away his family? *You're not wrong.* "In all this, Job did not sin or charge God with wrong" (Job 1:22).

Relationships, Not Just Reasons

Throughout the book of Job, a blameless and upright man groped for a reason, a purpose that could make sense of the sobering catastrophe he endured. God never offered him one.

In the search for a reason, Job's friends clung to the same formula we humans have clung to for ages: a human cause and a divine effect. They had no doubt Job's loss was a divine effect, so they assumed Job's sin must have been the human cause.

Job's friends didn't know about the conversation that happened in the first two chapters. They had not heard God's words to Satan, "Have you considered my servant Job, that there is none like him on the earth, a blameless and upright man, who fears God and turns away from evil?" (Job 1:8). In fact, without the first two chapters, *we* might have been tempted to join Eliphaz, Bildad, and Zophar in jumping to the conclusion Job was getting what his sins deserved!

Does God have reasons when he allows Satan to afflict us, his children? We believe he does. The biblical case is undeniable. God causes all things to work together for the good of those who love him (Romans 8:28). Christians throughout the centuries have clung to this assurance. When we suffer, God has a reason. It's for our good, and for his glory (Genesis 50:20).

However, as Job suffered, God offered him no such assurance. The only comment God made on the subject of *reasons* came in a conversation Job had no knowledge of. In chapter 2, God accused the accuser, saying, "you incited me against [Job] to destroy him *without reason*" (Job 2:3, italics added).

While his friends clung to their invented reasons, Job craved a deeper relationship with God. And while God remained silent about His reasons, He drew Job into a deeper relationship. Job's strong relationship with God sustained him through his suffering, even through the times he argued his case against God. His relationships with friends needlessly compounded his suffering.

For that reason, this small group study does not focus on the reasons God allows suffering in our lives. Instead, in keeping with the book of Job itself, the focus of this study is relationships. Our prayer is that God will use this study to draw you and your group into deeper relationships with one another, and, most of all, with Himself.

How to Use this Book

An Invitation To A Conversation

When Job spoke up about his sorrow, his so-called friends, Eliphaz, Bildad, and Zophar (along with the late-comer, Elihu) were outraged. They diagnosed the problem—Job was clearly a sinner. They corrected his theology—apparently Job did not know even the basic truths about God. And they prescribed a solution—Job should be quiet and repent of the sin he was surely hiding.

To make sure their friend got the point, they filled chapter after chapter bombarding Job with arguments, accusations, and advice.

If we're not careful, we might fall into the same trap. Imagine, instead, if we *learned* from the mistakes of Job's friends. As your group studies the book of Job, people who consider you a friend may find the courage to speak up about their own pain. When they do, you'll face a choice. Like Eliphaz, Bildad, and Zophar, you can choose to rebuke your friend's theology, diagnose their problem, and advise solutions. Or, you can choose to listen.

Handouts and Resources

If you are leading a group through this Bible study, you will need two resources:
1. *When Life Meets the Soul* by Ivan D. Parke (Morgan James, 2023), and
2. *When Life Meets the Soul Bible Study Guide* by Ivan D. Parke and Timothy J. Peabody (the book in your hand)

Participants in your group will also need two resources:
1. *When Life Meets the Soul* by Ivan D. Parke (Morgan James, 2023), and
2. Either:
   When Life Meets the Soul Bible Study Guide by Ivan D. Parke and Timothy J. Peabody (the book in your hand) or
   A copy of the free participant handouts at the back of this book

You will find handouts for each lesson at the back of this book. If you're leading a small group through this study, feel free to copy the handouts and distribute them to your group members. **You can also download a printable version of the handouts at ivanparke.com/resources.**

A Different Approach to Discussion Questions

Our prayer is that, as your group studies Job together, God will not only strengthen your relationship with Him, but also your relationships with one another. For this reason, we encourage you to allow plenty of time for discussion during your small group meetings.

Even if your group doesn't normally use discussion questions, we urge you to offer these questions to your group and listen closely to their answers. Each question has been carefully crafted, tested, and proven to accomplish its goal. When completed in order, they will allow your group members to not only study the Bible for themselves, but also discover *together* the meaning and application of each passage.

Each session begins with a question that's just for fun. We include that question because someone in your group may be trying to find the courage to speak up during Bible study. Even those who have no fear of speaking up sometimes need a little encouragement to get started. By cheerfully insisting *everyone answers the first question,* you will help your group get to know one another better, and you just might help someone find courage to speak up later when the topic of conversation turns to deeper matters.

We urge you to provide plenty of time for discussion as you complete this study. It would be a shame if, in our efforts to be right, we fell into the same trap that ensnared Eliphaz, Bildad, and Zophar—the trap of climbing on our soapbox when we could be listening to and comforting a suffering friend.

An Opportunity to Read the Entire Book of Job Together

Have you ever noticed that Job can be a difficult book to read? No one ever accused Eliphaz, Bildad, Zophar, and Elihu of being entertainers! However, we believe God chose to include these lengthy speeches in the Bible for a reason.

For centuries, public reading of Scripture was the only way Christians (and Jews before them) could experience the book of Job. Today, we are blessed with a high rate of literacy and unprecedented access to the Word of God. Yet each of us could testify to the unique power of God's words when they are read publicly in a group where two or more are gathered in His name.

Will you make an attempt to read the entire book of Job aloud together during your group study time?

We know Job is a long book. You might wonder, *could a small group possibly read 42 chapters in 10 weeks and still have time for teaching and discussion?* Good question!

Consider this. The entire book of Job has less than 19,000 words. At a moderate reading pace of 150 words per minute, you could read Job aloud in about 2 hours. That means, if your group spends an average of 13 minutes per week reading Job aloud, you could complete *the entire book* in 10 weeks and still have plenty of time for teaching and discussion.

Of course, some weeks reading the Bible passage will take longer than 15 minutes. Session 4 includes the longest readings (25 minutes). Sessions 5–9 each include about 20 minutes of reading from Job. For these longer sessions, we recommend choosing a reader who is comfortable reading at a faster pace.

Finally, don't get discouraged if you can't complete each of the recommended readings. When a session includes a longer Bible reading, we always include a shortened option that will give your group the essence of the Bible passage if you don't have time to read the longer passage.

May God bless you and your group as you complete this study of Job!

- Tim Peabody, September 15, 2022

Outline of Job

I. Prologue (Job 1:1–2:13)

II. Job's First Speech (Job 3)

III. Cycles of Dialogue (Job 4–27)

    1. Round One (Job 4–14)

    2. Round Two (Job 15–21)

    3. Round Three (Job 22–27)

IV. Wisdom Poem (Job 28)

V. Job's Final Speech (Job 29–31)

VI. Elihu's Speech (Job 32–37)

VII. Yahweh's Speeches (Job 38–41)

VIII. Job's Repentance and Restoration (Job 42)

Reading Plan

This small group study of Job was written to accompany *When Life Meets the Soul* (WLMTS) by Ivan D. Parke. The reading plan below allows your group to read the book of Job as you read *When Life Meets the Soul*.

Each week includes a small group session plus five daily readings. Some daily readings are from Job, and some are from *When Life Meets the Soul*. We recommend completing small group session 1 then starting the reading plan the following day.

You can also download a printable version of this reading plan at ivanparke. com/resources.

Schedule	Group Study	Daily Readings (begin after Session 1)	
Session 1	Job Worships in the Wake of Disaster (Job 1)		
Day 1		Job 1:1–2:10	☐
Day 2		WLMTS, Introduction	☐
Day 3		WLMTS, Chapter 1	☐
Day 4		WLMTS, Chapter 2	☐
Day 5		WLMTS, Chapter 3	☐
Session 2	Job Maintains His Integrity (Job 2:1–10)		
Day 6		Job 2:11–3:26	☐
Day 7		WLMTS, Chapter 4	☐
Day 8		WLMTS, Chapter 5	☐
Day 9		WLMTS, Chapter 6	☐
Day 10		WLMTS, Chapter 7	☐
Session 3	Job's Friends Begin Well (Job 2:11–3:26)		
Day 11		Job 4–5	☐
Day 12		Job 6–7	☐
Day 13		Job 15, Job 22	☐
Day 14		Job 23–24	☐
Day 15		WLMTS, Chapter 8	☐
Session 4	Eliphaz's Insults and Advice (Job 4–7, 15, 22–24)		
Day 16		Job 8–9	☐

Day 17		Job 10, 16–17	☐
Day 18		Job 18–19, 25	☐
Day 19		WLMTS, Chapter 9	☐
Day 20		WLMTS, Chapter 10	☐
Session 5	Bildad's Cause and Effect (Job 8–10, 16–19, 25)		
Day 21		Job 11–12	☐
Day 22		Job 13–14	☐
Day 23		Job 20	☐
Day 24		WLMTS, Chapter 11	☐
Day 25		WLMTS, Chapter 12	☐
Session 6	Zophar Makes It Personal (Job 11–14, 20)		
Day 26		Job 21, 26	☐
Day 27		Job 27–28	☐
Day 28		WLMTS, Chapter 13	☐
Day 29		WLMTS, Chapter 14	☐
Day 30		WLMTS, Chapter 15	☐
Session 7	Job Questions God (Job 21, 26–28)		
Day 31		Job 29–30	☐
Day 32		Job 31	☐
Day 33		WLMTS, Chapter 16	☐
Day 34		WLMTS, Chapters 17–18	☐
Day 35		WLMTS, Chapter 19	☐
Session 8	Job Tries to Force God to Answer (Job 29–31)		
Day 36		Job 32–33	☐
Day 37		Job 34–35	☐
Day 38		Job 36–37	☐
Day 39		WLMTS, Chapters 20–21	☐
Day 40		WLMTS, Chapters 22–23	☐
Session 9	Elihu Steps In (Job 32–37)		
Day 41		Job 38–39	☐
Day 42		Job 40–41	☐
Day 43		Job 42	☐
Day 44		WLMTS, Chapter 24	☐
Day 45		WLMTS, Chapter 25	☐
Session 10	God Answers Job (Job 38–42)		

S E S S I O N   1

Job Worships in the Wake of Disaster

Key Passage: Job 1

Passage Summary: Job worshiped God even when he lost everything.

Main Point: Even when tragedy strikes, we can worship God.

Applications from WLMTS: Chapter 1, "Give Me You: Being personal"
Value your relationship with God more than wealth or status (pp. 2-5).

Chapter 2, "Letting God Be God"
Avoid idolatry and think rightly about God (pp. 14-15).

Chapter 3, "Keeping What Matters"
Respond to personal loss by maintaining integrity and pursuing what lasts (pp. 21-24).

Opening Discussion

Question 1: What was the occupation of one of your grandparents or great-grandparents? *Everyone answers the first question. It's just for fun. And when you answer, say your name.*

_____

_____

_____

Question 2: Tell about an experience that made you think, "Wow! God is good."

_____

_____

_____

None Like Job

Job 1:1–12

> Have you considered my servant Job, that there is none like him on the earth? (Job 1:8)

Question 3: Let's read Job 1:1–12 and look for answers to this question: how was Job unique?

Read Job 1:1–12. *(3 minutes)*

_____

_____

_____

_____

Possible answers include:

He was "Blameless and upright" (Job 1:1).

He was very wealthy (Job 1:3).

He was diligent in offering sacrifices on behalf of his children (Job 1:5).

God said there was none like him (Job 1:8).

> **Over a lifetime (1:3), Job amassed a fortune because God had blessed him (1:9–10). Ascetics would expect Job to have been corrupted, to have become materialistic, but the books of Job and Ezekiel insist that the rich man from Uz was "blameless" and "upright" (1:1, 8; 2:3) and righteous (Ezekiel 14:12-20). In one afternoon, Job lost everything.** WLMTS, p. 19

Worship In The Wake Of Disaster

Job 1:13–22

Question 4: Let's read Job 1:13–22 and list the disasters that fell on Job.

Possible answers include:

Enemies took his oxen and donkeys and killed his servants (Job 1:14–15).

"Fire from heaven" killed his sheep and other servants (Job 1:16).

Enemies took his camels and killed still more servants (Job 1:17).

"A great wind" destroyed the house his children were in, killing them all (Job 1:18–19).

Read Job 1:13–22. *(2 minutes)*

> **Job suffered material loss (lots of livestock)–that which can be replaced–and personal loss (ten children)–that which cannot be replaced. Immediately afterwards, he worshiped, declaring "The Lord has taken away" (Job 1:21). What Job said reflected his worldview: God is the cause, not God is culprit.** WLMTS, p. 21

When we face suffering, we don't always know God's reasons. The narrator of the book let us know what prompted Job's suffering: a conversation between God and Satan. In the conversation, God celebrated Job's uprightness, but Satan cast suspicion on Job's motives.

> Satan, a Hebrew noun, means "adversary." It appears twenty-seven times in the Old Testament, fourteen times in Job. Seven times, satan refers to a human being (1 Samuel 29:4; 2 Samuel 19:22; 1 Kings 5:4; 11:14, 23, 25; Psalm 109:6). WLMTS, p. 7

Despite the fact he knew nothing about this conversation between God and Satan, Job worshiped the Lord and did not charge God with wrong.

> Then Job arose and tore his robe and shaved his head and fell on the ground and worshiped. And he said, "Naked I came from my mother's womb, and naked shall I return. The Lord gave, and the Lord has taken away; blessed be the name of the Lord." In all this Job did not sin or charge God with wrong. (Job 1:20–22)

Question 5: Verse 22 says, "In all this Job did not sin or charge God with wrong." If Job were going to "charge God with wrong," what might he say?

_____

_____

_____

When we read Job's words in verse 21, we might be tempted to argue with him. *Technically, Job, God didn't take away your household…Satan did.* However, the narrator assured us that, in saying this, "Job did not sin or charge God with wrong" (Job 1:22).

Apply the Passage

Even when tragedy strikes, we can worship God.

Question 6: As God said in verse 8, there was no one like Job in all the earth. It's easy to see how Job was different from us; but can you think of anything we have in common with him?

_____

_____

_____

> Although we cannot meet him face-to-face, two facts characterize Job and us. Fact #1: All of us are a lot alike. Fact #2: Each of us is unique. WLMTS, p. xxiii

Question 7: Tell about a time you saw tragedy shake a person's faith in God.

_____

_____

_____

Question 8: Tell about an experience that shook your faith that God is good or made you wonder whether He loved you.

_____

_____

_____

Question 9: What is one experience you hope our study of Job might help you understand or overcome?

_____

_____

_____

Closing Prayer: Father, You are worthy of our worship. Teach us to worship You even when we face tragedy. Amen.

> On mountaintops or through valleys, to live well is to walk with God. No exceptions. In your life, is spiritual intimacy a memory, a reality, or a goal? WLMTS, p. xxvi

SESSION 2

Job Maintains His Integrity

Key Passage: Job 2:1–10

Passage Summary: Job did not curse God, even when Satan incited God against him for no reason.

Main Point: We can maintain our integrity and our faith even when God does not explain the reasons for our suffering.

Applications from WLMTS: Introduction
"To live well is to walk with God" (p. xxvi).

Chapter 3, "Keeping What Matters"
Resist the conclusion God has mistreated you (p. 23).

Opening Discussion

Question 1: What food did you learn to like as you got older? *Everyone answers the first question. It's just for fun. And when you answer, say your name.*

_____

_____

_____

Question 2: Tell about a time you saw someone worship God through tragedy.

_____

_____

_____

Worship Without Reasons

We can maintain our integrity and our faith even when God does not explain the reasons for our suffering. In Job 2:1–10, even after Job's suffering increased, he did not accuse God of wrong.

In our last session, we read about four disasters that struck Job:
- Enemies took his oxen and donkeys and killed his servants (Job 1:14–15).
- "Fire from heaven" killed his sheep and other servants (Job 1:16).
- Enemies took his camels and killed still more servants (Job 1:17).
- "A great wind" destroyed the house his children were in, killing them all (Job 1:18–19).

In the chapter we'll read today, Job's life got even worse. The adversary doubled down his assault on Job's integrity saying, "Stretch out your hand and touch his bone and his flesh, and he will curse you to your face" (Job 2:5). For a second time, God permitted Satan to afflict Job. As a result, Job's entire body was covered with sores (Job 2:7–8). Still, Job refused to speak a word against God.

Question 3: Let's read Job 2:1–10 and list the questions God asked and the boundaries He placed on Job's suffering.

Read Job 2:1–10. *(3 minutes)*

_____

_____

_____

_____

Possible answers include:

"From where have you come?" (Job 2:2).

"Have you considered my servant Job…" (Job 2:3).

"Only spare his life" (Job 2:6).

Question 4: In Job 2:10, Job said, "Shall we receive good from God, and shall we not receive evil?" What about Job's question might bother a person?

_____

_____

_____

The Temptation to Curse God

Job 2:1–10

> Then his wife said to him, "Do you still hold fast your integrity? Curse God and die." But he said to her, "You speak as one of the foolish women would speak. Shall we receive good from God, and shall we not receive evil?" In all this Job did not sin with his lips. (Job 2:9–10)

Question 5: Have you ever seen a person respond to tragedy by cursing God?

_____

_____

_____

In verse 9, Job's wife said to him, "Curse God and die." This marks the fourth time in two chapters we have encountered the idea of cursing God.

Job feared that his children, despite their prosperous and harmonious lives, might curse God in their hearts. "And when the days of the feast had run their course, Job would send and consecrate them, and he would rise early in the morning and offer burnt offerings according to the number of them all. For Job said, 'It may be that my children have sinned, and cursed God in their hearts.' Thus Job did continually" (Job 1:5).

Twice Satan suspected suffering might prompt Job to curse God. "But stretch out your hand and touch all that he has, and he will curse you to your face" (Job 1:11). "But stretch out your hand and touch his bone and his flesh, and he will curse you to your face" (Job 2:5).

Finally, even Job's wife urged him to curse God. "Then his wife said to him, 'Do you still hold fast your integrity? Curse God and die'" (Job 2:9).

We saw in chapter 1 that Job's continual burnt offerings were prompted by the possibility that his children had "sinned, and cursed God in their hearts" (Job 1:5). As Job's words implied, cursing God is not always a visible act; a person might curse God without speaking a word. Or, as the prophet Isaiah put it, a person might pay lip service to God "while their hearts are far from me" (Isa. 29:13).

> **Did anyone offer himself or herself to Job? His wife did not. She advised Job, 'Curse God and die!' (2:9b)—her last words in the story.**
> WLMTS p.2

Question 6: Do you see a difference between cursing God in your heart and being angry with God?

_____

_____

_____

Question 7: How could Job's experience help you face tragedy without "cursing God"?

_____

_____

_____

Closing Prayer: Father, help us to maintain our faith and integrity even when we don't understand why we're suffering. Amen.

SESSION 3

Job's Friends Begin Well

Key Passage: Job 2:11–3:26

Passage Summary: Job's friends wept and sat silently with him until he cursed the day he was born.

Main Point: When comforting a suffering friend, silent presence is better than careless words.

Applications from WLMTS: Chapter 4, "Handling Chronic Pain: When God Chooses Not to Heal" When asking for healing, pray, "God, grow me during trials and God, glorify yourself through afflictions" (p. 30).

Chapter 5, "Time Out: Addressing the Elephant in the Room" Remember that reasons are not enough to comfort a suffering person (p. 44).

Chapter 6, "Knowing How to Minister" When comforting a suffering friend, be careful what you say, and don't worry about what your friend says (p. 49).

Chapter 7, "Being Honest with God" "God can handle our honesty. He would rather us turn to Him in rage than turn our backs to Him with a respectful, stifled silence" (p. 59).

> Tragedy... unites us and divides us. Of course, it unites us because heartbreak doesn't discriminate. We all have a "story." It also divides us into two categories whenever someone's everything falls apart: sufferers and comforters. WLMTS, p. 45

Opening Discussion

Question 1: Tell us about a time you realized you had a good friend.
Everyone answers the first question. It's just for fun. And when you answer, say your name.

_____

_____

_____

Question 2: Tell about a time somebody tried to make you feel better, but it didn't help.

_____

_____

_____

When comforting a suffering friend, silent presence is better than careless words. As we read today's passage, we'll explore two roles each of us will play at some point in our life: the sufferer and the comforter.

The Silence of a Comforter

Job 2:11–13

> **If you're the sufferer, don't worry about what you say. If you're the comforter, be careful about what you say.** WLMTS, p. 49

Question 3: In Job 2:11–13, what did Job's friends do when they heard about his suffering?

Read Job 2:11–13. *(1 minute)*

_____

_____

Job's friends seemed to start so well! In Job 2:11–13, they wept and sat silently with him. However, in chapter 3, Job cursed the day he was born. When they heard his bitter words, they began an argument that would go on for 24 chapters! Instead of comforting their suffering friend, they added to his pain.

> The Hebrew verb nud, translated 'sympathize,' depicts a back and forth movement, aptly describing a sympathizer shaking his head compassionately or grieving with a quivering lip (Job 16:5). The Hebrew verb nacham, translated 'comfort,' originally indicated 'breathing deeply...the physical display of one's feelings.' Both verbs also appear together in 42:11. WLMTS, p. 46 (citing Theological Wordbook of the Old Testament, vol. II; Gesenius' Hebrew-Chaldee Lexicon to the Old Testament)

The Words of a Sufferer

Job 3:1–26

> After each round of testing, Job's respect for God's sovereignty did not waver. He even worshiped God as he mourned the death of his children. How he behaved warranted what the narrator and God had attested: "That man was blameless, upright, fearing God, and turning away from evil." (Job 1:1, 8; 2:3) Beginning with the First Monologue, Job's attitude changed drastically. Criticism of God supplanted his esteem for God. WLMTS, p. 52

The narrator of Job assured us twice that Job's initial response to tragedy was good (Job 1:22; 2:10). The narrator's declarations of Job's innocence apply to everything Job said in the prologue (chapters 1–2), but not everything he said in the chapters that follow. Starting in chapter 3, "A seismological shift had occurred in Job's worldview: God became culprit" (WLMTS, p. 23).

Job 3 is a dark chapter. As we read the words Job spoke in his grief, we might find points of disagreement. We don't have to agree with everything Job said in his grief, but God does expect us to hear what Job said.

Question 4: Let's read Job 3:1–26 and list the questions Job asked.

Read Job 3:1–26. *(4 minutes)*

Possible answers include.

"Why did I not die at birth, come out from the womb and expire?" (Job 3:11).

"Why did the knees receive me? Or why the breasts, that I should nurse?" (Job 3:12).

"Or why was I not as a hidden stillborn child, as infants who never see the light?" (Job 3:16).

"Why is light given to him who is in misery…who long for death…and are glad when they find the grave?" (Job 3:20–22).

"Why is light given to a man whose way is hidden, whom God has hedged in?" (Job 3:23).

_____

_____

_____

_____

_____

_____

_____

_____

What did Job's friends expect him to say? Judging by their response in the chapters to come, we can assume Job's friends expected him to confess his sins. When his words did not meet their expectations, they revealed what miserable comforters they truly were.

> The friends soon failed to do what they had intended to do. The Cycles of Dialogue reveal why. They, during their silence, had judged Job. They then waited for a confession of sins…. When Job cursed the day of his birth … Censuring and silencing Job replaced sympathizing and comforting him. WLMTS, p. 46

Question 5: What did Job say that might cause his friends to argue with him on theological grounds?

_____

_____

_____

Apply the Passage

Sitting silently with someone who suffers is better than throwing out careless words.

In our first session, we asked a very personal question: *Have you ever experienced something that shook your faith that God is good or made you wonder whether he loved you?*

We're going to ask that question again. Before we do, let's all agree that, if someone shares an answer, we will just sit silently. If we feel the need to say anything at all, we'll just say, "I'm sorry." We don't want to make the same mistake Job's friends made and debate with you about your pain. So here's the question again:

Question 6: Have you ever experienced something that shook your faith that God is good or made you wonder whether he loved you?

_____

_____

_____

Allow plenty of time for your group to answer question 6. If time allows, invite your group to continue studying by comparing Job's statement of grief in chapter 3 to the words of other grievers in the Bible:
- Psalm 10:1–2
- Psalm 39:12–13
- Psalm 44:20–26
- Jeremiah 20:7–8; 14–18

Closing Prayer: Father, thank You for the comfort we find in You. Teach us to offer true comfort to those we know who face suffering. Amen.

SESSION 4

Eliphaz's Insults and Advice

Key Passage: Job 4–7, 15, 22–24

Passage Summary: Eliphaz insisted God was punishing Job, but Job protested.

Main Point: We cannot comfort a suffering person with insults and advice.

Applications from WLMTS: Chapter 8, "Leaving it Blank"
Resist the urge to assume you know the reasons for God's actions.

Opening Discussion

Question 1: Who was your best friend when you were eight years old? *Everyone answers the first question. It's just for fun. And when you answer, say your name.*

_____

_____

_____

Question 2: Tell about a time you thought you were getting what you deserved.

_____

_____

_____

We cannot comfort a suffering person with insults and advice. After the tragedies Job suffered in chapters 1 and 2, his friends came to comfort him. However, when Job cursed the day of his birth, they could no longer be silent.

Eliphaz was the first of Job's friends to speak. He insisted God was punishing Job, but Job protested. Eliphaz's speeches are recorded in chapters 4, 5, 15, and 22. As time allows, we'll read his speeches today plus some of Job's responses.

Eliphaz's Insults and Advice

Job 4–5, 15, & 22

Instead of comforting his friend, Eliphaz pelted Job with a barrage of insults and advice. At first, Eliphaz's insults were subtle and masked with religious words.

> Remember: who that was innocent ever perished?
>   Or where were the upright cut off?
> As I have seen, those who plow iniquity
>   And sow trouble reap the same.
> By the breath of God they perish,
>   And by the blast of his anger they are consumed. (Job 4:7–9)

But soon Eliphaz removed the veil from his accusations. By chapter 22, his insults were blunt and exaggerated.

> Is not your evil abundant?
>   There is no end to your iniquities. (Job 22:5)

Question 3: As we read Job 4–5, let's list the insults and advice Eliphaz offered to Job.

Read Job 4–5. *(6 minutes)*
If time allows, also read Job 15 and Job 22. *(9 minutes)*

_____

_____

_____

_____

_____

_____

_____

_____

_____

_____

_____

_____

Possible answers include:

Implied insult: "You have instructed many…But now it has come to you…" (Job 4:3–5).

Insult: "you are impatient… dismayed" (Job 4:5).

Implied insult: "who that was innocent ever perished?" (Job 4:6–9).

Implied insult: "Can mortal man be in the right before God?" (Job 4:17).

Advice: "Call now; is there anyone who will answer you? To which of the holy ones will you turn?" (Job 5:1).

Implied insult: "Surely vexation kills the fool, and jealousy slays the simple" (Job 5:2).

Implied insult: "I have seen the fool taking root, but suddenly I cursed his dwelling. His children are far from safety; they are crushed in the gate…" (Job 5:3–4). (Job's children were just crushed to death in Job 1:19!)

Advice: "As for me, I would seek God, and to God would I commit my cause" (Job 5:8).

Advice: "Behold, blessed is the one whom God reproves; therefore despise not the discipline of the Almighty" (Job 5:17).

Advice: "Behold, this we have searched out; it is true. Hear, and know it for your good" (Job 5:27).

_____

_____

_____

_____

_____

_____

Job's Criticism

Job 6–7, & 23–24

> Is there any injustice on my tongue?
>   Cannot my palate discern the cause of calamity? (Job 6:30)

Question 4: Let's read Job 7 and 24 and list ways Job criticized God.

Read Job 7 and Job 24. *(4 minutes)*
If time allows, also read Job 6 and Job 23. *(6 minutes)*

Possible answers include:

"You scare me with dreams and terrify me with visions" (Job 7:14).

"How long will you not look away from me, nor leave me alone till I swallow my spit? If I sin, what do I do to you, you watcher of mankind? Why have you made me your mark? Why have I become a burden to you?" (Job 7:19–20).

"From out of the city the dying groan, and the soul of the wounded cries for help; yet God charges no one with wrong" (Job 24:12).

_____

_____

_____

_____

_____

_____

_____

_____

_____

Job's friends seemed to believe sin was the only legitimate explanation for suffering. However, Chapter 5 of *When Life Meets the Soul* identifies six biblical answers to the question of suffering (pp. 38–43).

"They wrong the barren, childless woman, and do no good to the widow. Yet God prolongs the life of the mighty by his power; they rise up when they despair of life" (Job 24:21–22).

Six Biblical Reasons for Suffering

- Testing of One's Faith
- Consequences of Sinfulness
- Sanctification
- Getting One's Attention
- Glorifying God
- Consequences of Living in a Fallen World

Question 5: Identify which of the six reasons you see in each of the following passages.

> "But stretch out your hand and touch his bone and his flesh, and he will curse you to your face." And the Lord said to Satan, "Behold, he is in your hand; only spare his life." (Job 2:5–6)

_____

> You have sent widows away empty,
>   and the arms of the fatherless were crushed.
> Therefore snares are all around you,
>   and sudden terror overwhelms you. (Job 22:9–10)

_____

> But he knows the way that I take;
>   when he has tried me, I shall come out as gold. (Job 23:10)

_____

> Man is also rebuked with pain on his bed
>   and with continual strife in his bones. (Job 33:19)

_____

> Narrators are fundamental to narrative. They tell the story and interact with readers. In the book of Job, the narrator is unrestricted spatially. He travels freely in the Prologue between heaven and earth as he escorts readers. We, therefore, know why Job suffers. None of the earthly characters ever do, but the words "I don't know" never come out of their mouth. Their lips dripped with confidence. WLMTS, p. 62

Apply the Passage

We cannot comfort a suffering person with insults and advice. When Eliphaz tried, God rebuked him by name.

> After the Lord had said these things to Job, he said to Eliphaz the Temanite, "I am angry with you and your two friends, because you have not spoken the truth about me, as my servant Job has." (Job 42:7)

> How God regards false prophets explains His rebuke of Eliphaz, Bildad, and Zophar: "My anger burns against you and against your two friends, for you have not spoken of me what is right as my servant Job has" (Job 42:7 ESV). WLMTS, p. 192

Question 6: Why do you think God rebuked Eliphaz but not Job?

_____

_____

_____

> Do you think that you can reprove words,
>   when the speech of a despairing man is wind? (Job 6:26)

Question 7: We know more about the reasons for Job's suffering than he did. How do you think it would have changed Job's experience if he had known what we know?

_____

_____

_____

Question 8: We also know more about the reasons for Job's suffering than his friends did. How do you think it would have changed their response if Job's friends had known what we know?

_____

_____

_____

Question 9: How could these chapters change the way you respond to your own suffering or the suffering of others?

_____

_____

_____

Closing Prayer: Father, even when reasons fail to comfort, teach us to find comfort in You and to offer comfort to others.

SESSION 5

Bildad's Cause and Effect

Key Passage: Job 8–10, 16–19, 25

Passage Summary: When Bildad urged Job to repent, Job pleaded his case with God and despaired at God's silence.

Main Point: When God seems silent, we should resist the temptation to assume we know his reasons. Instead we can put our hope in Christ, our Mediator, who never leaves us.

Applications from WLMTS: Chapter 9, "Waiting When God is Silent"
When you experience the silence of God's "waiting room," continue praying with faith that God's silence is not "apathy, inactivity, or absence" (p. 74).

Chapter 10, "Welcoming God's Imperceptible Presence"
Remember that God "never abandons us during life's darkest moments" (p. 83).

Opening Discussion

Question 1: Where do you like to go when you need silence? *Everyone answers the first question. It's just for fun. And when you answer, say your name.*

_____

_____

_____

Question 2: Tell about a time you felt like God was silent.

_____

_____

_____

After the tragedies of chapters 1 and 2, Job's friends, Eliphaz, Bildad, and Zophar traveled to comfort him. However, when Job cursed the day he was born (Job 3), his friends could remain silent no longer. They began bombarding him with accusations, insults, and advice. Last week we read Eliphaz's speeches and some of Job's responses.

This week we'll read what Job's second friend, Bildad, said. Like Eliphaz, Bildad assumed he knew the cause of Job's suffering—Job was suffering because Job had sinned. When Bildad urged Job to repent, Job pleaded his case with God and despaired at God's silence.

Bildad's Cause and Effect

Job 8, 18, & 25

Bildad loved human causes paired with divine effects. For example, in Job 8:4, he said, "If your children have sinned against him, he has delivered them into the hand of their transgression." Like Eliphaz and Zophar, Bildad was dogmatic about the cause and effect relationship between human sin and divine punishment.

> **Eliphaz, Bildad, or Zophar could have been the poster child for dogmatism. They put God in a theological box, the doctrine of divine retribution.** WLMTS, p. 87

Behold, even the moon is not bright,
    and the stars are not pure in his eyes;
how much less man, who is a maggot,
    and the son of man, who is a worm!" (Job 25:5–6)

Question 3: As we read Bildad's speeches in Job 8, 18, and 25, let's list the human causes and divine effects Bildad focused on.

Read Job 8, Job 18, and Job 25. *(6 minutes)*

_____

_____

_____

_____

_____

_____

_____

_____

_____

_____

Possible answers include:

"If your children have sinned against him, he has delivered them into the hand of their transgression" (Job 8:4).

"If you will seek God and plead with the Almighty for mercy, if you are pure and upright, surely then he will rouse himself for you and restore your rightful habitation" (Job 8:5–6).

"Such are the paths of all who forget God; the hope of the godless shall perish" (Job 8:13).

"Behold, God will not reject a blameless man, nor take the hand of evildoers" (Job 8:20).

"Indeed, the light of the wicked is put out, and the flame of his fire does not shine" (Job 18:5–21).

Eliphaz, Bildad, and Zophar had relied upon their theology, the doctrine of divine retribution. It convinced them that Job was wicked because, according to their beliefs, the wicked always suffer. God judges them. WLMTS, pp. 103-104

Job's Question

Job 9–10

Question 4: As we read Job's words in chapter 9, let's list the things he felt powerless to do. For example, in Job 9:11, Job felt powerless to see God.

Read Job 9–10. *(8 minutes)*

Possible answers include:

"be in the right before God?" (Job 9:2)

"contend with [God]" or "answer him" (Job 9:3)

"perceive him" (Job 9:11)

"say to him, 'What are you doing?'" (Job 9:12)

"answer him" (Job 9:14–15)

Justify or defend himself against God (Job 9:20)

Forget his complaint or cheer up (Job 9:27)

Cleanse himself (Job 9:30–31)

Speak without fear (Job 9:35)

_____

_____

_____

_____

_____

_____

_____

_____

Question 5: In Job 9:2, Job surprised us by agreeing with Bildad! Which of Bildad's statements in chapter 8 do you think Job might agree with?

_____

_____

_____

Hope for a Mediator

Job 16, 17, and 19

Did Job believe he was sinless? He repeatedly declared he was innocent. We might get the impression Job thought he was sinless.

However, at times Job's words revealed an awareness of his own sin. For example, in Job 13:26 (ESV), he said, "For you write bitter things against me and make me inherit the iniquities of my youth." (See also Job 10:14 & 14:14.)

> **The fate of the wicked was also a topic in six of Job's speeches … he insisted that his suffering was not deserved punishment but mistreatment by an unjust God who also allows the wicked to live carefree.** WLMTS, p. 104

Job's awareness of his own sin would explain his question at the beginning of chapter 9. "How can a man be in the right before God?" (Job 9:2)

We've seen this question before. In Job 4:17, Eliphaz asked, "Can mortal man be in the right before God? Can a man be pure before his Maker?" And again in chapter 15, he said, "What is man, that he can be pure? Or he who is born of a woman, that he can be righteous?" (Job 15:14). Bildad asked the same question in chapter 25, verse 4: "How then can man be in the right before God? How can he who is born of woman be pure?"

Question 6: How would you answer Job's question in chapter 9, verse 2? "How can a man be in the right before God?" (Job 9:2b)

_____

_____

_____

As Christians, we know the answer to Job's question is Christ—His death and resurrection atoned for our sin, providing the way for sinners to become righteous by faith in Him. Job lived long before Christ, but he was aware of his need for a "mediator between God and men" (1 Tim. 2:5). He acknowledged that need when he said, "There is no arbiter between us, who might lay his hand on us both." (Job 9:33)

Question 7: As we read Job 16:11–17:16 and Job 19:11–29, let's look for times Job's words suggested the need for an arbiter or mediator.

Read Job 16:11–17:16 and Job 19:11–29 *(6 minutes)*
If time allows, read all of Job 16, 17, and 19. *(9 minutes)*

Possible answers include:

"My eye pours out tears to God, that he would argue the case of a man with God" (Job 16:20 –21).

"Who is there who will put up security for me?" (Job 17:3).

"Who will see my hope? Will it go down to the bars of Sheol? Shall we descend together into the dust?" (Job 17:15–16).

"For I know that my Redeemer lives … and after my skin has been thus destroyed, yet in my flesh I shall see God" (Job 19:15–26).

_____

_____

_____

_____

_____

_____

_____

_____

Apply the Passage

Question 8: How might Job's experience change if he knew more about the coming arbiter, Jesus Christ?

_____

_____

_____

Question 9: How can a relationship with Christ change the experience of suffering for us?

_____

_____

_____

Closing Prayer: Father, give us the faith to wait humbly when You seem silent. Thank You for Christ, our mediator. Amen.

Faith quashes the hysteric assumption that God's silence is apathy, inactivity, or absence. Prayer keeps the lines of communication open; attuning our attention when He does answer. WLMTS, p. 74

SESSION 6

Zophar Makes It Personal

Key Passage: Job 11–14, 20

Passage Summary: When Zophar attacked Job with insults, Job took his case to God.

Main Point: We can be honest with God when life doesn't make sense.

Applications from WLMTS: Chapter 11, "Rejecting Pessimism: A Box without God"
Choose a God-centered realism rather than concluding God won't or can't change your situation (p. 93).

Chapter 12, "Contending with Criticism"
When critics attack, keep your focus on God and his mission (p. 99).

Opening Discussion

Question 1: Tell us about a time you knew you were right. *Everyone answers the first question. It's just for fun. And when you answer, say your name.*

_____

_____

_____

Question 2: Have you ever talked with someone who believed God had done them wrong? What did they say?

_____

_____

_____

Zophar Makes It Personal

Job 11 and Job 20

After Job's series of tragedies, Zophar was the third friend to speak. It should come as no surprise that Zophar agreed with Eliphaz and Bildad on the main point: Job was getting the punishment his sins deserved.

But, according to Zophar, not only did Job deserve what he got—he deserved even worse! "Know then," Zophar said to Job, "that God exacts of you less than your guilt deserves." (Job 11:6)

We might ask Zophar, *how could things possibly get any worse for Job?* Zophar provided the answer: "When you mock, shall no one shame you?" (Job 11:3). Job's life could be worse if his friends shamed him, so Zophar gave Job what he thought he deserved. From Zophar's warped perspective, on top of all Job endured, he deserved even more insults from his alleged friends!

Question 3: As we read Job 11 and Job 20, let's list the ways Zophar shamed Job.

Read Job 11 and Job 20. *(7 minutes)*

_____

_____

_____

_____

_____

_____

_____

_____

_____

_____

_____

Possible answers include:

He called Job "a man full of talk" and called his words "babble" (Job 11:1–2).

He assumed he knew more about God than Job did (Job 11:5–6).

He implied Job was stupid (Job 11:12–12).

He assumed Job needed to repent (Job 11:13–14).

He brought up the blemishes on Job's face and assumed (wrongly) they were the the result of Job's sin (Job 11:15).

He implied Job was wicked and warned him about the fate of the wicked (Job 11:20).

He continued elaborating on the fate of the wicked, warning Job that tragedies like those Job endured are "the wicked man's portion from God" (Job 20:29).

Chapter 20 contains Zophar's second speech. In this speech, he eased up on the insults, but not before claiming *he* was the one being insulted (Job 20:3).

> I hear censure that insults me. (Job 20:3)

Zophar's main focus in chapter 20 was the fate of the wicked. He insisted the wicked may appear to prosper for a moment, but their prosperity is always short-lived. "The exulting of the wicked is short," he assured Job (Job 20:5).

> Do you not know this from of old,
>   since man was placed on earth,

> that the exulting of the wicked is short,
>   and the joy of the godless but for a moment? (Job 20:4–5)

Throughout the chapter he described many disasters similar to Job's tragedy and claimed with great confidence such disasters were the "wicked man's portion from God" (Job 20:29).

Job's Lawsuit

Job 12–14

We can be honest with God when life doesn't make sense. When Zophar attacked Job with insults, Job took his case to God.

Job's lawsuit against God leveled two charges (WLMTS, p. 70):
- Charge #1: God abuses his power. God's omnipotence was Job's theme in chapter 12. Job observed that God does anything He wants, even pouring contempt on princes (Job 12:21). The implication was that God was responsible for Job's suffering. "Who among all these does not know that the hand of the Lord has done this?" he asked in Job 12:9 (ESV).
- Charge #2: God ignores wickedness. Chapter 12 also contains the second charge in Job's lawsuit: God ignores the sins of the wicked, allowing them to prosper despite their rebellion. "The tent of robbers are at peace, and those who provoke God are secure," Job complained (Job 12:6). In our next session, we'll read chapter 21 in which Job elaborates on his charges related to the prosperity of the wicked.

In addition to charges, Job's lawsuit also made requests, asking both God and his friends to respond in specific ways.

Question 4: As we read Job 13 and 14, let's identify the charges and requests Job made.

Read Job 13–14. *(7 minutes)*
If time allows, also read Job 12. *(3 minutes)*

Possible answers include:

Request: to speak to God (Job 13:3).

Charge: his friends are worthless physicians and liars (Job 13:4).

_____

_____

_____

_____

_____

_____

_____

_____

_____

_____

_____

_____

_____

_____

_____

_____

_____

_____

_____

_____

_____

_____

Request: that his friends would keep silent and listen (Job 13:5–6, 13, 17).

Charge: his friends speak falsely and show partiality when they defend God (Job 13:7–11).

Charge: the maxims and defenses of his friends are worthless (Job 13:12).

Request: that God "withdraw your hand far from me, and let not dread of you terrify me" (Job 13:21).

Request: that God would reply and tell Job what his sins are (Job 13:22–24).

Charge: God makes "me inherit the sins of my youth" (Job 13:26).

Charge: God limits Job's steps and makes him waste away (Job 13:27–28).

Request: Because you have appointed the limits on unclean man, "look away from him and leave him alone" (Job 14:4–6).

Request: "Oh that you would hide me in Sheol, that you would conceal me until your wrath be past … and remember me!" (Job 14:13).

(Continued opposite)

Request:"You would call, and I would answer you; you would long for the work of your hands." (Job 14:15).

Request: "… you would not keep watch over my sin; my

transgression would be sealed up in a bag, and you would cover over my iniquity" (Job 14:16–17).

_____

_____

Take note of the request Job made in Job 14:15–17. In these verses, he pleaded for forgiveness and a restored relationship. He asked that God "would not keep watch over my sin; my transgression would be sealed up in a bag, and you would cover over my iniquity."

This plea for forgiveness might surprise us in light of the many times Job defended his innocence. However, these verses serve as another reminder that Job was not sinless (Job 10:14, Job 13:26).

Like each of us, Job needed forgiveness, and he needed to know God loved him.

Apply the Passage

> Let me have silence, and I will speak,
> and let come on me what may.
> Why should I take my flesh in my teeth
> and put my life in my hand?
> Though he slay me,
> I will hope in him;
> yet I will argue my ways to his face. (Job 13:13–15)

Job's lawsuit included many *charges* and *requests*, but chapters 13 and 14 also included many questions. Consider the following *questions* Job asked God:
- "How many are my iniquities and my sins?" (Job 13:23).
- "Why do you hide your face and count me as your enemy?" (Job 13:24).
- "And do you … bring me into judgment with you?" (Job 14:3).
- "Who can bring a clean thing out of an unclean?" (Job 14:4).
- "If a man dies, shall he live again?" (Job 14:14)

Question 5: Tell us about a time you were glad you asked God a question.

_____

_____

_____

Asking God a question is nothing to take lightly. Even a righteous man like Job felt he was taking his life in his hands when he argued his ways to God's face (Job 13:14–15). However, Job managed to gather his courage to speak, "let come on me what may" (Job 13:14).

Even John the Baptist had a question for Jesus. The question he asked in Matthew 11:3 might surprise you.

> When Jesus had finished instructing his twelve disciples, he went on from there to teach and preach in their cities. Now when John heard in prison about the deeds of the Christ, he sent word by his disciples and said to him, "Are you the one who is to come, or shall we look for another?" (Matthew 11:1–3)

The road named "Doubt" winds through pessimism and skepticism and ends at cynicism. The cynic, unlike the believer, couldn't care less. During the Cycles of Dialogue, despair drove Job to pessimism but no farther because God intervened, contacting him from the whirlwind. WLMTS, p. 88

Before we ask the next question, I'd like us all to agree that, for now, we will just listen to each other instead of trying to provide answers to a question somebody else brings up. Agreed?

Question 6: What question would you ask God if you could ask Him anything?

_____

_____

_____

Closing Prayer: Father, thank You for the privilege of speaking to You and even asking You questions. Teach us to cling to You even when we don't understand Your ways. Amen.

SESSION 7

Job Questions God

Key Passage: Job 21, 26–28

Passage Summary: Job could not understand why a just God would punish a righteous man.

Main Point: When we don't understand God's plan, we can take our questions to Him, but we should keep in mind that we don't know the entire story.

Applications from WLMTS: Chapter 13, "Balancing Short-Term and Long-Term"
Keep your focus on the eternal by faith and the practice of the spiritual disciplines (pp. 106–07).

Chapter 14, "Appreciating and Applying Amazing Grace"
"Whenever we live beyond what is fair, our 'righteousness surpasses that of the scribes and Pharisees'" (WLMTS, p. 116; Matt. 5:20; NASB).

Chapter 15, "Acquiring Wisdom"
Wisdom is found in God, and its foundation is the fear of the Lord.

Opening Discussion

Question 1: What helps you concentrate? *Everyone answers the first question. It's just for fun. And when you answer, say your name.*

_____

_____

_____

Question 2: Tell about a time you saw somebody succeed when they deserved to fail.

_____

_____

_____

Why Do the Wicked Prosper?

Job 21

The debate continues between Job and his friends. Job could not understand why a just God would punish a righteous man. Job's frustration was compounded by the apparent prosperity of the wicked.

> **When he compared his condition to the well-being of the wicked around him, Job floundered.** WLMTS, p. 103

In chapter 20, Zophar tried to explain the prosperity of the wicked by claiming their prosperity is only temporary. "The exulting of the wicked is short," he explained (Job 20:5). Chapter 21 contains Job's response.

> Why do the wicked live, reach old age,
>   and grow mighty in power? (Job 21:7)

In response, Job cited the evidence of his own eyes. Don't tell Job the prosperity of the wicked is short lived—Job had seen the wicked "reach old age, and grow mighty in power" (Job 21:7). If Zophar refused to believe Job's testimony, he should listen to the stories of travelers who would report "that the evil man is spared in the day of calamity, that he is rescued in the day of wrath" (Job 21:30).

Job ended chapter 21 with disgust: "How then will you comfort me with empty nothings? There is nothing left of your answers but falsehood" (Job 21:34).

Question 3: Let's read Job 21 and list the questions Job asked God about the prosperity of the wicked.

Read Job 21. *(4 minutes)*

_____

_____

_____

_____

_____

_____

_____

_____

_____

_____

Possible answers include:

"Why do the wicked live, reach old age, and grow mighty in power?" (Job 21:7).

"Behold, is not their prosperity in their hand?" (Job 21:16).

How often is their lamp put out? (Job 21:17–18).

"What do they care for their houses after them when the number of their months is cut off?" (Job 21:21).

"Will any teach God knowledge, seeing that he judges those who are on high?" (Job 21:22).

"Who declares his way to his face, and who repays him for what he has done?" (Job 21:31).

Two Truths and a Lie?

Job 26–28

As we reach the end of the "Cycles of Dialogue" (Job 4–27), we might struggle to make sense of the often repetitive, sometimes contradictory, and seemingly endless debates. However, if we step back, we can see that the essence of these chapters is a competition between three seemingly incompatible beliefs.

Three *Seemingly* Incompatible Beliefs:
- God was the cause of Job's suffering.
- God punishes the wicked and rewards the righteous.
- Job was righteous.

Job's friends abandoned the third belief. In order to defend God's justice, they jumped to the conclusion that Job *deserved* his tragedies. His suffering was all the evidence they needed—surely God would only send such tragedies to a wicked person. According to Eliphaz, Bildad, and Zophar, the lie was belief number three—Job was *not* righteous.

> Is it for your fear of him that he reproves you
> and enters into judgment with you?
> Is not your evil abundant?
> There is no end to your iniquities. (Job 22:4–5)

Job, on the other hand, assumed the lie must be belief number two—God must *not* be just. In Job's case, it seemed God had punished the righteous.

> I am blameless;
> I regard not myself;
> I loathe my life.
> It is all one; therefore I say,
> "He destroys both the blameless and the wicked." (Job 9:21–22)

It's somewhat surprising that neither Job nor his friends questioned the first belief. We've seen Job's friends question Job's righteousness. We've seen Job question God's justice. Yet they were unanimous that God was the cause of Job's suffering.

> As God lives, who has taken away my right,
> and the Almighty, who has made my soul bitter, as long as my
> breath is in me,
> and the spirit of God is in my nostrils, my lips will not speak
> falsehood,
> and my tongue will not utter deceit. Far be it from me to say
> that you are right;
> till I die I will not put away my integrity from me. I hold fast
> my righteousness and will not let it go;
> my heart does not reproach me for any of my days. (Job 27:2–6)

As we read Job 26, we'll see that Job had full confidence that God is the cause of everything that happens. "The thunder of his power who can understand?" Job asked (Job 26:14). In fact, Job 26:5–14 bears a striking resemblance to the lecture on divine power God himself delivered in chapters 38–39.

Question 4: As we read Job 26 and 27, let's listen for times Job's words sounded like something his friends would say.

Read Job 26–27. *(5 minutes)*
If time allows, also read Job 28. *(4 minutes)*

_____

_____

_____

> Job's third response to Bildad (chaps. 26-27) seems contradictory. It concludes with a graphic account of God punishing the wicked (27:13-23). Why would Job criticize God as unjust throughout the Cycles of Dialogue, even in 27:2, but affirm Him as just in 27:13-23? Because Job's closing remarks sound just like the friends, some Old Testament scholars (e.g., Marvin Pope, H. H. Rowley, and Norman Habel) seize 27:13-23 in order to create a third speech for Zophar. The verses that precede 27:13-23, however, help to interpret it. Job chastised the friends in verses 7-12. He called them "enemy" and "opponent" (27:7). Their folly warranted God's judgment which Job then describes in verses 13-23. This eleven-verse section, therefore, should be read as critical of the friends, not complimentary of God. WLMTS, p. 104

In chapter 28, the narrator changed the subject from the prosperity of the wicked to the quest for wisdom, devoting 11 verses to the long and difficult task of mining for gold and precious jewels. If gold and sapphires are worth such effort, how much more is wisdom worth searching out? Wisdom is harder to find than gold, but it is more valuable too.

Apply the Passage

When we don't understand God's plan, we can take our questions to Him. However, we should keep in mind that we are not God, and we do not know the entire story.

> Christians, despite having the right answers, struggle much with the problem of evil.... What makes a trying situation tougher is not knowing which of the biblical answers apples when it matters most: in the throes of agony. Job's reality was worse; he never knew why. WLMTS, pp. 43-44

Question 5: Do you think it would have helped if Job had known the reason for his suffering?

_____

_____

_____

Question 6: Tell about a time you were confident you knew the reason for your suffering

_____

_____

_____

Question 7: In your experience, does it help to know the reasons for your suffering?

_____

_____

_____

Closing Prayer: Father, You are in control, and You are good. Help us to trust You when we don't understand. Keep us from assuming we know the reasons for another person's tragedy. Amen.

SESSION 8

Job Tries to Force God to Answer

Key Passage: Job 29–31

Passage Summary: In an attempt to force God to respond, Job unleashed a series of oaths, calling down God's judgment upon himself if he had not lived an innocent life.

Main Point: Taking our frustrations to God can be good, but we cannot force God to respond.

Applications from WLMTS: Chapter 16, "Rethinking Trials and Tragedies"
We can thank God when He uses adversity to reveal and strengthen our character (p. 130).

Chapter 17, "Seeing Worth from God's Viewpoint"
When we find our identity in God, we can avoid pride and self-centeredness (p. 139).

Chapter 18, "Not Forcing the Issue: How Right Becomes Wrong"
"To do what is right honors God and helps others. Self-righteousness, on the other hand, is self-serving" (p. 144).

Chapter 19, "Approaching God on His Terms"
Instead of trying to force God's hand with bluster and bargaining, we should humbly approach God's throne asking for mercy through Christ.

> Job's test was unique... Initially, Job did well... Ultimately, Job did well... For a while, however, Job languished. The test exposed the anger, pride, disrespect, and self-righteousness that lurked in his heart. WLMTS, pp. 129-30

Opening Discussion

Question 1: What is a challenge most people don't realize you're facing? *Everyone answers the first question. It's just for fun. And when you answer, say your name.*

_____

_____

_____

Question 2: Tell about a time you tried to force God to act or speak.

_____

_____

_____

Job's attempt to convince God to speak came to a climax in chapters 29–31 where he presented his case in extreme terms. In his closing arguments, Job remembered how good his life was (Job 29) and how unbearable it had become (Job 30). Finally, in an attempt to force a response from God, Job unleashed a series of oaths, calling down judgment on himself if he had not lived an innocent life (Job 31).

Our previous sessions have included about 400 verses of Job's words. Throughout his speeches, Job defended his uprightness and pleaded his case. Think back on the many times Job begged God to speak. For example:
- "Let me know why you contend against me" (Job 10:2).
- "Who is there who will contend with me?" (Job 13:19).
- "Let me speak, and you reply to me" (Job 13:22).
- "Why do you hide your face and count me as your enemy?" (Job 13:24).
- "Oh, that I knew where I might find him … I would know that he would answer me" (Job 23:3–5).

Remembering the Good Old Days

Job 29

In chapter 29, Job remembered (with possible exaggeration) how good his life was "when the friendship of God was upon my tent" (Job 29:4). In those blissful days, Job's reputation for good deeds caused even princes to fall silent in his presence (Job 29:9–12).

Question 3: As we read Job 29, let's list the good deeds Job was known for back when he enjoyed "the friendship of God" (Job 29:4).

Read Job 29. *(3 minutes)*

_____

_____

_____

_____

_____

_____

_____

_____

_____

_____

Possible answers include:

He delivered the poor and the fatherless (Job 29:12).

He brought comfort to the dying and joy to widows (Job 29:13).

"I put on righteousness…my justice was like a robe and a turban" (Job 29:14).

"I was eyes to the blind and feet to the lame. I was a father to the needy" (Job 29:15–16).

"I searched out the cause of him whom I did not know" (Job 29:16).

"I broke the fangs of the unrighteous and made him drop his prey from his teeth" (Job 29:17).

He counseled men (Job 29:21).

"I smiled on them when they had no confidence" (Job 29:24).

He was "like one who comforts mourners" (Job 29:25).

From Cause to Culprit

Job 30

From the beginning, Job expressed no doubt God was the *cause* of his disaster. To his credit, Job did not blame the Lord. In the early chapters, Job saw God as the cause, but not the *culprit* (WLMTS, p. 21). "The Lord gave, and the Lord has taken away; blessed be the name of the Lord" (Job 1:21).

However, as time dragged on and God remained silent, Job's opinion of God's justice began to change. By chapter 30, Job was openly criticizing God's justice. "You have turned cruel to me," he cried, "with the might of your hand you persecute me" (Job 30:21).

Once a "father to the needy" (Job 29:16), Job was now the butt of their jokes. "And now I have become their song," he lamented. "They do not hesitate to spit at the sight of me" (Job 30:9–10). As he mourned how far he had fallen, it became clear Job saw himself as a victim—not only a victim of the rabble (Job 30:12), but also a victim of God.

Question 4: As we read Job 30, let's list the actions Job believed God had taken against him.

Read Job 30. *(4 minutes)*

Possible answers include:

"God has loosed my cord and humbled me" (Job 30:11).

"God has cast me into the mire" (Job 30:19).

"I cry to you for help and you do not answer me; I stand, and you only look at me" (Job 30:20).

"You have turned cruel to me; with the might of your hand you persecute me" (Job 30:21).

"You lift me up on the wind; you make me ride on it, and you toss me about in the roar of the storm." (Job 30:22).

"I know that you will bring me to death" (Job 30:23).

_____

_____

_____

_____

_____

_____

_____

_____

Forcing the Issue

Job 31

By the time we arrive at Job's final speech, it is clear Job saw himself as unquestionably right. Chapter 31 contains several oaths that follow a two-part formula.

The Two-Part Formula of Job's Oaths in Chapter 31:
- **Part 1: If I have sinned…**
  For example, "If I have walked with falsehood…" (Job 31:8).
- **Part 2: then let disaster strike me.**
  For example, "…then let me sow, and another eat" (Job 31:8).

Question 5: As we read Job 31, let's list the sins Job claimed to be innocent of.

Read Job 31. *(4 minutes)*

_____

_____

_____

_____

_____

_____

_____

_____

_____

Possible answers include:

Gazing at a virgin (Job 31:1).

Falsehood and deceit (Job 31:5).

"If my step has turned aside from the way and my heart has gone after my eyes, and if any spot has stuck to my hands" (Job 31:7).

"If my heart has been enticed toward a woman, and I have lain in wait at my neighbor's door" (Job 31:9).

"If I have rejected the cause of my manservant or my maidservant, when they brought a complaint against me" (Job 31:13).

"If I have withheld anything that the poor desired, or have caused the eyes of the widow to fail, or have eaten my morsel alone, and the fatherless has not eaten of it" (Job 31:16–17).

> **To prove how righteous he was ... Job forced the issue, filing a lawsuit against God. His case rested upon God being guilty. In the court of public opinion, he pressured God to apologize; one of his tactics was flaunting his own righteousness.** WLMTS, p. 142

As we read chapter 31, some of Job's oaths might cause us to cringe. Could any man possibly be as righteous as Job claimed to be? Does he not share our belief that "all have sinned and fall short of the glory of God" (Romans 3:23)?

After all, Job's self-righteous words resemble the prayer of the pharisee in Luke 18 (WLMTS, p. 132). The pharisee prayed, "God, I thank you that I am not like other men, extortioners, unjust, adulterers, or even like this tax collector. I fast twice a week; I give tithes of all that I get" (Luke 18:11–12).

Jesus condemned the attitude of the pharisee: "For everyone who exalts himself will be humbled, but the one who humbles himself will be exalted" (Luke 18:14).

Question 6: How would it change your impression of Job if chapter 31 were the first chapter in the book?

_____

_____

_____

Would Jesus condemn Job's attitude in chapter 31?

If we speculate on the question, we should remember two facts from the book of Job. First, God did not hesitate to call Job "a blameless and upright man who fears God and turns away from evil" (Job 1:8, 2:3). Second, God responded to Job's words more favorably than he responded to the words of Job's friends. In fact, God's harsh words to Eliphaz included a defense of Job's words: "My anger burns against you and against your two friends, for you have not spoken of me what is right, as my servant Job has" (Job 42:7, italics added).

As we will see in session 10, Job received his share of sternness from God. Starting in chapter 38, God silenced him with questions like "Who is this that darkens counsel by words without knowledge?" (Job 38:2) and "Shall a faultfinder contend with the Almighty?" (Job 40:2).

If Job's words in chapter 31 sound self-righteous, we can safely conclude they _are_ self-righteous. However, when God finally chose to respond to Job's accusations, Job let go of his self-righteousness. He humbled himself confessing, "I have uttered what I did not understand," (Job 42:3) and "I despise myself, and repent in dust and ashes" (Job 42:6).

Question 7: Chapters 29–31 describe a time when Job's relationship with God was strained. Still, do you see in these chapters any sign of strength in Job's relationship with God?

_____

_____

_____

> [Job] couldn't intimidate God with legal action or impress Him by touting his righteous past. What Job wanted (exoneration) was less than what he got (more unconditional love) when God revealed himself freely from the whirlwind. WLMTS, p. 152

Apply the Passage

Question 8: What are some of the ways we try to force God to respond?

_____

_____

_____

Question 9: It's likely that, at some point, every one of us will feel desperate for God to respond. How can a relationship with Jesus change that experience?

_____

_____

_____

Closing Prayer: Father, we pray that our relationship with you will sustain us through times of desperation. Thank you for the hope we have in Christ and the presence of your Spirit in our lives. Amen.

SESSION 9

Elihu Steps In

Key Passage: Job 32–37

Passage Summary: After Job tried to force God to speak, the newcomer Elihu offered more speeches, shifting attention to God's goodness.

Main Point: Life requires patience because our words and actions cannot coerce God to speak or act.

Applications from WLMTS: Chapter 20, "Emulating Elihu"
"I want to be like Elihu, ready to talk about my God and capable of turning an ordinary conversation into spiritual contemplation" (p. 159).

Chapter 21, "Celebrating God is Free"
We can approach God as he is, without attempting to corner or manipulate him (p. 168).

> **Job must have been disappointed to hear the voice of another human being, but Elihu's appearance spoke volumes. Job learned what sovereignty means. God cannot be coerced, ever. Job's drastic measures secured none of his demands: he had wanted Yahweh; he got Elihu!** WLMTS, p. 158

Opening Discussion

Question 1: Tell about a time you were so thirsty that water tasted amazing. *Everyone answers the first question. It's just for fun. And when you answer, say your name.*

_____

_____

_____

Question 2: Tell about a time you had to wait for God.

_____

_____

_____

Introducing...Elihu?

Job 32

We've read 29 chapters of speeches from Job and his friends. When we finally arrive at the end of Job's words, the book takes a surprising turn. Instead of a response from God, Job got four speeches from Elihu, a man we never met before chapter 32, a man who is never listed among Job's friends.

Question 3: As we read Job 32, let's list answers to this question: what motivated Elihu to speak up?

Read Job 32. *(3 minutes)*

_____

_____

_____

_____

_____

_____

_____

_____

_____

_____

Possible answers include:

"He burned with anger at Job because he justified himself rather than God" (Job 32:2).

"He burned with anger also at Job's three friends because they had found no answer, although they had declared Job to be in the wrong" (Job 32:3).

It is the spirit of God, not age that give wisdom (Job 32:7–10).

"There was none among you who refuted Job or who answered his words" (Job 32:12).

He didn't want Job's friends to assume they had won the argument because no one answered them (Job 32:13–16).

He was ready to burst (Job 32:18–20).

Let's Hear Him Out

Job 33–37

When he finally spoke up, Elihu made a poor first impression. Apparently he had been listening silently while Job, Eliphaz, Bildad, and Zophar made their speeches (Job 32:2–5). His long introduction (Job 32:6–33:7) comes off as "brash and abrasive" (WLMTS, p. 156).

However, Elihu succeeded in one thing: he turned the topic of conversation from the fate of the wicked to the "goodness, righteousness, and creative power" of God (WLMTS, p. 158).

Question 4: As we read Job 33–34, let's answer this question: How did Elihu summarize Job's words?

Read Job 33–34. *(8 minutes)*
If time allows, also read Job 35–37. *(8 minutes)*

Possible answers include:

"You say, 'I am pure, without transgression; I am clean, and there is no iniquity in me. Behold, he finds occasions against me, he counts me as his enemy, he puts my feet in the stocks and watches all my paths.'" (Job 33:9–11).

"Why do you contend against him, saying, 'He will answer none of man's words'?" (Job 33:13).

"For Job has said, 'I am in the right, and God has taken away my right; in spite of my right I am counted a liar; my wound is incurable, though I am without transgression'" (Job 34:5–6).

He thinks Job is a scoffer who travels in the company of evil men (Job 34:7–8).

"For he has said, 'It profits a man nothing that he should take delight in God'" (Job 34:9).

"He answers like wicked men. For he adds rebellion to his sin; he claps his hands among us and multiplies his words against God'" (Job 34:36–37).

_____

_____

_____

_____

_____

_____

_____

_____

_____

_____

_____

_____

Giving Elihu a Chance

> Most Old Testament scholars have not been kind to Elihu.... According to them, Elihu talked big (impetuous) but failed to deliver.... Even though Elihu talked a lot, he did not add anything to the discussion (unoriginal). After he finally finished, no one responded positively or negatively (ineffectual). WLMTS, pp. 155–56

What did God think about Elihu's speeches? Eliphaz, Bildad, and Zophar received a rebuke from God in Job 42:7. Job even received a rebuke in Job 38:2 (though he also received an affirmation in Job 42:7). Elihu, however, received neither a rebuke nor an affirmation from God. It is worth noting that the speeches of Job and his friends failed to prompt an immediate response from God. It was not until Elihu finished that God finally spoke up (WLMTS, p. 159).

Question 5: Let's look again at Job 33:23–30. Which phrases in this section remind you of your own experience with Christ?

Read Job 33:23–30. *(2 minutes)*

_____

_____

_____

> The memorized theology of Job's friends did not prod God. Job's antics certainly didn't. Only Elihu was God's herald: whetting appetites with a foretaste of the divine; preparing hearts for worship. WLMTS, p. 159

Apply the Passage

Question 6: Does Elihu offer any example you would like to imitate?

_____

_____

_____

Question 7: Based on what we've learned in previous sessions, would you offer Elihu any suggestions for comforting a suffering person?

_____

_____

_____

> Behold, we consider those blessed who remained steadfast. You have heard of the steadfastness of Job, and you have seen the purpose of the Lord, how the Lord is compassionate and merciful. (James 5:11)

> Like any question, "why" fosters listening because it fine-tunes attention: the expectation of an answer. Hope sustains patience until the answer hopefully comes. WLMTS, p. 188

Question 8: What will you remember about Job when you find yourself waiting on God?

_____

_____

_____

Closing Prayer: Father, we worship You for Your goodness, glory, and power. Give us patience when we desperately want answers but they do not come.

S E S S I O N   1 0

God Answers Job

Key Passage: Job 38–42

Passage Summary: When God finally answered Job, Job repented. God then rebuked Job's friends and restored Job.

Main Point: A relationship with God makes it possible to worship Him, even when He doesn't answer all our questions.

Applications from WLMTS: Chapter 22, "Responding Well When God Confronts"
When God confronts us, the appropriate response is humble repentance (pp. 179–80).

Chapter 23, "Distinguishing Knowledge and Answers"
"Job could have rejected God's speeches as words but not answers because God did not say what he had wanted to hear. Instead, Job worshiped again" (p. 188).

Chapter 24, "Thinking before Speaking: 'Thus Saith the Lord'"
Knowing God does not give us the right to presume we know why God acts in another person's life (p. 194).

Chapter 25, "Testifying God is Still in Control"
When we find ourselves "atop the ash heap," we can testify, "God is in control" (p. 204).

Opening Discussion

Question 1: What is your favorite comeback story? *Everyone answers the first question. It's just for fun. And when you answer, say your name.*

_____

_____

_____

Question 2: Tell about a time God answered you in a way you didn't expect.

_____

_____

_____

God Answers Job Out of the Whirlwind

Job 38-41

In the final chapters of Job, God answered Job out of the whirlwind with a four-chapter barrage of questions.

> Who is this that darkens counsel
>   by words without knowledge?
> Dress for action like a man;
>   I will question you, and you make it known to me.
> Where were you when I laid the foundation of the earth?
>   Tell me, if you have understanding (Job 38:2–4).

> Will you even put me in the wrong? Will you condemn me that
>   you may be in the right? (Job 40:8).

Question 3: As we read Job 38 and Job 40, let's list the types of questions and challenges God confronted Job with.

Read Job 38 and Job 40. *(7 minutes)*
If time allows, also read Job 39 and 41. *(7 minutes)*

_____

_____

_____

_____

_____

_____

_____

_____

_____

Possible answers include:

He challenged Job to answer a series of questions only God knows the answer to (Job 38:3–11, 28–30, 33).

He challenged Job to answer questions that reminded Job he did not have the power God had (Job 38:3–11, 19–21, 25–27, 36–41).

He asked Job if he could do things God alone can do (Job 38:12–18, 22–24, 31–35).

He asked whether Job was capable of judging the world rightly (Job 40:2, 6–14).

He asked Job whether Job could capture with a snare Behemoth which God created (Job 40:15–24).

> **God did answer: two lengthy replies. Neither speech, however, met Job's expectations. God never addressed any of Job's whys… He did not tackle the topic of suffering.** WLMTS, p. 186.

Question 4: How was God's response different from the response Job expected?

_____

_____

_____

Job Retracts His Lawsuit

Job 42:1–6

When God spoke, Job responded with humility and repentance. "I have uttered what I did not understand," he confessed (Job 42:3). He went on to retract his lawsuit against God: "I had heard of you … but now my eye sees you; therefore I despise myself and repent in dust and ashes" (Job 42:5–6).

Read Job 42:1–6. *(2 minutes)*

> **Job's response to the Second Yahweh Speech concluded with an unconditional surrender: "I take back everything I said, and I sit in dust and ashes to show my repentance" ([Job 42:6], NLT) .**
>
> **The first verb in verse 6 is transitive. "Transitive" grammatically refers to a verb whose action involves a direct or indirect object or both, but an object does not follow ma'as, translated "take back" (NLT), "retract" (NASB), "reject" (CSB), "abhor" (KJV, NKJV), or "despise" (NIV). English translators supply one.**
> **I take back everything I said (NLT).**
> **I reject my words (CSB).**
> **I abhor myself (KJV, NKJV).**
> **I despise myself (NIV).**
>
> **In English Bibles, the direct object "everything I said," "words," or "myself" will be italicized because it does not occur in the original (Hebrew) text. Albeit implied, the better reading of verse 6 is that Job retracted his lawsuit. His charges had been baseless, tainted by ulterior motive: a failed attempt to manipulate God.** WLMTS, p. 179.

God Restores Job

Job 42:7–17

Read Job 42:7–9. *(1 minute)*

God rebuked Eliphaz, Bildad, and Zophar saying, "You have not spoken of me what is right as my servant Job has" (Job 42:7). He commanded them to take seven bulls and seven rams and go to Job so he could offer sacrifices and a prayer on their behalf. The three friends "did what the LORD had told them, and the LORD accepted Job's prayer" (Job 42:9).

Read Job 42:10–17. *(2 minutes)*

Finally, God restored Job's fortunes. He restored Job's wealth, his family, his livestock, and his friends. The book concludes with the following summary:

> And after this Job lived 140 years, and saw his sons, and his son's sons, four generations. And Job died, an old man, and full of days. (Job 42:16–17)

Apply the Passage

Question 5: Why do you think God chose not to give Job any reason for the suffering he endured?

_____

_____

_____

Question 6: How do you think Job changed after his experience with God?

_____

_____

_____

God restored many things to Job, but not everything. We don't know whether God restored Job's health (WLMTS, p. 29). Furthermore, many things Job lost on that tragic day in chapter 1 were irreplaceable.

Remember, Job didn't lose possessions and livestock only—he lost *people*. In chapter 31, Job described the deep love and respect he held for the people around him, including even the servants in his household (Job 31:13). Job would have been grieved by their loss. How much more would he have felt the pain of losing all ten of his children? No matter how much he loved the children God brought him later in life, the scars would have remained.

The people he lost were irreplaceable, but Job lost something else that day that he could never regain: he lost his belief that fearing God would insulate him from tragedy. When it came to fearing God, no one on earth surpassed Job (Job 1:8). Like Job and his friends, we would assume such uprightness would guarantee God's protection. It did not.

In the first chapter, Satan leveled the accusation that Job feared God only because God protected him—remove that protection, and "He will curse you to your face" (Job 1:11). When God removed Job's protection, Job floundered. As Job realized his fear of God would not protect him from disaster, he wondered if there was any point at all in fearing God. By chapter 23, his fear of God was nothing more than terror and dread in the presence of the one who does what he desires and has "many such things" in mind (Job 23:14).

By the end of the book, Job's fear of God had not failed, but it had changed. He retained a relationship with God, but he shed the belief that his relationship with God would shield him from suffering.

Jesus told us to look to the sparrow because He wanted us to live without fear, not because the sparrow never falls.

> Oftentimes, our assessment of the situation lacks key facts, inaccessible for a lot of reasons. Case in point, Job. He yearned for the perspective that we the readers have at our fingertips: specifically, the Prologue. Even when God spoke from the whirlwind, He withheld information that Job would have appreciated. Our ongoing challenge whenever the senseless or unthinkable happens is not to jump to conclusions but to remind ourselves that God is still in control. Hasn't He earned the benefit of the doubt? WLMTS, p. 202

Question 8: How has our study of Job changed you?

_____

_____

_____

Closing Prayer: Father, teach us to cling to You and trust in You when we can't see the reasons for our suffering. Thank You for the example we have in Job, the hope we have in Jesus, and the comfort we have in Your Spirit. Amen.

Handouts

Download printable handouts for free at ivanparke.com/resources.

HANDOUT FOR SESSION 1

Job Worships in the Wake of Disaster

Key Passage: Job 1

Passage Summary: Job worshiped God even when he lost everything.

Main Point: Even when tragedy strikes, we can worship God.

Opening Discussion

Question 1: What was the occupation of one of your grandparents or great-grandparents?

_____

_____

_____

Question 2: Tell about an experience that made you think, "Wow! God is good."

_____

_____

_____

None Like Job

Job 1:1–12

Have you considered my servant Job, that there is none like him on the earth? (Job 1:8)

Question 3: Read Job 1:1–12 and list answers to this question: how was Job unique?

_____

_____

_____

Worship in the Wake of Disaster

Job 1:13–22

Question 4: Read Job 1:13–22 and list the disasters that fell on Job.

_____

_____

_____

When we face suffering, we don't always know God's reasons. The narrator of the book let us know what prompted Job's suffering: a conversation between God and Satan. In the conversation, God celebrated Job's uprightness, but Satan cast suspicion on Job's motives.

Despite the fact he knew nothing about this conversation between God and Satan, Job worshiped the Lord and did not charge God with wrong.

> Then Job arose and tore his robe and shaved his head and fell on the ground and worshiped. And he said, "Naked I came from my mother's womb, and naked shall I return. The Lord gave, and the Lord has taken away; blessed be the name of the Lord." In all this Job did not sin or charge God with wrong. (Job 1:20–22)

Question 5: Verse 22 says, "In all this Job did not sin or charge God with wrong." If Job were going to "charge God with wrong," what might he say?

_____

_____

_____

H A N D O U T   F O R   S E S S I O N   2

Job Maintains His Integrity

Key Passage: Job 2:1–10

Passage Summary: Job did not curse God, even when Satan incited God against him for no reason.

Main Point: We can maintain our integrity and our faith even when God does not explain the reasons for our suffering.

Opening Discussion

Question 1: What food did you learn to like as you got older?

_____

_____

_____

Question 2: Tell about a time you saw someone worship God through tragedy.

_____

_____

_____

Worship Without Reasons

We can maintain our integrity and our faith even when God does not explain the reasons for our suffering. In Job 2:1–10, even after Job's suffering increased, he did not accuse God of wrong.

Question 3: Read Job 2:1–10 and list the questions God asked and the boundaries He placed on Job's suffering.

_____

_____

_____

Question 4: In Job 2:10, Job said, "Shall we receive good from God, and shall we not receive evil?" What about Job's question might bother a person?

_____

_____

_____

The Temptation to Curse God

In verse 9, Job's wife said to him, "Curse God and die." This marks the fourth time in two chapters we have encountered the idea of cursing God.

> And when the days of the feast had run their course, Job would send and consecrate them, and he would rise early in the morning and offer burnt offerings according to the number of them all. For Job said, "It may be that my children have sinned, and cursed God in their hearts." Thus Job did continually. (Job 1:5)

> But stretch out your hand and touch all that he has, and he will curse you to your face. (Job 1:11)

> But stretch out your hand and touch his bone and his flesh, and he will curse you to your face. (Job 2:5)

> Then his wife said to him, "Do you still hold fast your integrity? Curse God and die." (Job 2:9)

As Job's words implied, cursing God is not always a visible act; a person might curse God without speaking a word. Or, as the prophet Isaiah put it, a person might pay lip service to God "while their hearts are far from me" (Isa. 29:13).

HANDOUT FOR SESSION 3

Job's Friends Begin Well

Key Passage: Job 2:11–3:26

Passage Summary: Job's friends wept and sat silently with him until he cursed the day he was born.

Main Point: When comforting a suffering friend, silent presence is better than careless words.

> Tragedy ... unites us and divides us. Of course, it unites us because heartbreak doesn't discriminate. We all have a "story." It also divides us into two categories whenever someone's everything falls apart: sufferers and comforters. WLMTS, p. 45

Opening Discussion

Question 1: Tell us about a time you realized you had a good friend.

_____

_____

_____

Question 2: Tell about a time somebody tried to make you feel better, but it didn't help.

_____

_____

_____

The Silence of a Comforter

Job 2:11–13

When comforting a suffering friend, silent presence is better than careless words. As we read today's passage, we'll explore two roles each of us will play at some point in our life: the sufferer and the comforter.

Question 3: Read Job 2:11–13, what did Job's friends do when they heard about his suffering?

_____

_____

_____

The Words of a Sufferer

Job 3:1–26

Question 4: Read Job 3:1–26 and list the questions Job asked.

_____

_____

_____

What did Job's friends expect him to say? Judging by their response in the chapters to come, we can assume Job's friends expected him to confess his sins. When his words did not meet their expectations, they revealed what miserable comforters they truly were.

Question 5: What did Job say that might cause his friends to argue with him on theological grounds?

_____

_____

_____

HANDOUT FOR SESSION 4

Eliphaz's Insults and Advice

Key Passage: Job 4–7, 15, 22–24

Passage Summary: Eliphaz insisted God was punishing Job, but Job protested.

Main Point: We cannot comfort a suffering person with insults and advice.

Opening Discussion

Question 1: Who was your best friend when you were eight years old? *Everyone answers the first question. It's just for fun. And when you answer, say your name.*

_____

_____

_____

Question 2: Tell about a time you thought you were getting what you deserved.

_____

_____

_____

Eliphaz's Insults and Advice

Job 4–5, 15, & 22

Question 3: Read Job 4–5 and list the insults and advice Eliphaz offered to Job.

_____

_____

_____

Job's criticism

Job 6–7, & 23–24

Question 4: Read Job 7 and 24 and list ways Job criticized God.

_____

_____

_____

Six Biblical Reasons for Suffering

1. Testing of One's Faith
2. Consequences of Sinfulness
3. Sanctification
4. Getting One's Attention
5. Glorifying God
6. Consequences of Living in a Fallen World

Question 5: Which of the six reasons for suffering do you see in each of the passages below?

"But stretch out your hand and touch his bone and his flesh, and he will curse you to your face." And the Lord said to Satan, "Behold, he is in your hand; only spare his life." (Job 2:5–6)

You have sent widows away empty,
    and the arms of the fatherless were crushed.
Therefore snares are all around you,
    and sudden terror overwhelms you. (Job 22:9–10)

But he knows the way that I take;
    when [God] has tried me, I shall come out as gold. (Job 23:10)

Man is also rebuked with pain on his bed
    and with continual strife in his bones. (Job 33:19)

HANDOUT FOR SESSION 5

Bildad's Cause and Effect

Key Passage: Job 8–10, 16–19, 25

Passage Summary: When Bildad urged Job to repent, Job pleaded his case with God and despaired at God's silence.

Main Point: When God seems silent, we should resist the temptation to assume we know his reasons.

Opening Discussion

Question 1: Where do you like to go when you need silence?

_____

_____

_____

Question 2: Tell about a time you felt like God was silent.

_____

_____

_____

Bildad's Cause and Effect

Job 8, 18, & 25

Like Eliphaz, Bildad assumed he knew the cause of Job's suffering—Job was suffering because Job had sinned. Bildad loved human causes paired with divine effects. For example, in Job 8:4 (ESV), he said, "If your children have sinned against him, he has delivered them into the hand of their transgression." When Bildad urged Job to repent, Job pleaded his case with God and despaired at God's silence.

Question 3: As we read Bildad's speeches in Job 8, 18, and 25, let's list the human causes and divine effects Bildad focused on.

_____

_____

_____

Job's question

Job 9–10

Question 5: Read Job's words in Job 9 & 10 and list the things he felt powerless to do. For example, in Job 9:11, Job felt powerless to see God.

_____

_____

_____

Hope for a Mediator

Job 16, 17, and 19

Question 7: Read Job 16, 17, and 19 then list times Job's words suggested the need for an arbiter or mediator.

_____

_____

_____

HANDOUT FOR SESSION 6

Zophar Makes It Personal

Key Passage: Job 11–14, 20

Passage Summary: When Zophar attacked Job with insults, Job took his case to God.

Main Point: We can be honest with God when life doesn't make sense.

Opening Discussion

Question 1: Tell us about a time you knew you were right.

_____

Question 2: Have you ever talked with someone who believed God had done them wrong? What did they say?

_____

Zophar Makes It Personal

Job 11 and Job 20

After Job's series of tragedies, Zophar was the third friend to speak. It should come as no surprise that Zophar agreed with Eliphaz and Bildad on the main point: Job was getting the punishment his sins deserved.

But, according to Zophar, not only did Job deserve what he got—he deserved even worse! "Know then," Zophar said to Job, "that God exacts of you less than your guilt deserves." (Job 11:6)

Know then, that God exacts of you less than your guilt deserves. (Job 11:6)

We might ask Zophar, how could things possibly get any worse for Job? Zophar provided the answer: "When you mock, shall no one shame you?" (Job 11:3). Job's life could be worse if his friends shamed him, so Zophar gave Job what he thought he deserved. From Zophar's warped perspective, on top of all Job endured, he deserved even more insults from his alleged friends!

Question 3: Read Job 11 and Job 20, then list the ways Zophar shamed Job.

_____

_____

_____

Job's Lawsuit

Job 12–14

Question 4: Read Job 13 and 14, let's identify the charges and requests Job made.

_____

_____

_____

> Let me have silence, and I will speak,
>   and let come on me what may.
> Why should I take my flesh in my teeth
>   and put my life in my hand?
> Though he slay me,
>   I will hope in him;
>   yet I will argue my ways to his face. (Job 13:13–15)

Take note of the request Job made in Job 14:15–17. In these verses, he pleaded for forgiveness and a restored relationship. He asked that God "would not keep watch over my sin; my transgression would be sealed up in a bag, and you would cover over my iniquity."

This plea for forgiveness might surprise us in light of the many times Job defended his innocence. However, these verses serve as another reminder that Job was not sinless (Job 10:14, Job 13:26).

Like each of us, Job needed forgiveness, and he needed to know God loved him.

HANDOUT FOR SESSION 7

Job Questions God

Key Passage: Job 21, 26–28

Passage Summary: Job could not understand why a just God would punish a righteous man.

Main Point: When we don't understand God's plan, we can take our questions to Him, but we should keep in mind that we don't know the entire story.

Opening Discussion

Question 1: What helps you concentrate?

_____

_____

_____

Question 2: Tell about a time you saw somebody succeed when they deserved to fail.

_____

_____

_____

Why Do the Wicked Prosper?

Job 21

The debate continues between Job and his friends. Job could not understand why a just God would afflict a righteous man. Job's frustration was compounded by the apparent prosperity of the wicked.

In chapter 20, Zophar tried to explain the prosperity of the wicked by claiming their prosperity is only temporary. "The exulting of the wicked is short," he explained (Job 20:5). Chapter 21 contains Job's response.

> Why do the wicked live, reach old age,
> and grow mighty in power? (Job 21:7)

Question 3: Read Job 21 and list the questions Job asked God about the prosperity of the wicked.

_____

_____

_____

Two Truths and a Lie?

Job 26–28

Three Seemingly Incompatible Beliefs
1. God was the cause of Job's suffering.
2. God punishes the wicked and rewards the righteous.
3. Job was righteous.

Job's friends rejected belief number three.

> Is it for your fear of him that he reproves you
> and enters into judgment with you?
> Is not your evil abundant?
> There is no end to your iniquities. (Job 22:4–5)

Job rejected belief number two.

> I am blameless;
> I regard not myself;
> I loathe my life.
> It is all one; therefore I say,
> "He destroys both the blameless and the wicked." (Job 9:21–22)

Question 4: Read Job 26 and 27. What did Job say that sounds like something his friends would say?

_____

_____

_____

HANDOUT FOR SESSION 8

Job Tries to Force God to Answer

> **Key Passage:** Job 29–31
>
> **Passage Summary:** In an attempt to force God to respond, Job unleashed a series of oaths, calling down God's judgment upon himself if he had not lived an innocent life.
>
> **Main Point:** Taking our frustrations to God can be good, but we cannot force God to respond.

Opening Discussion

Question 1: What is a challenge most people don't realize you're facing?

_____

_____

_____

Question 2: Tell about a time you tried to force God to act or speak.

_____

_____

_____

Job's attempt to convince God to speak came to a climax in chapters 29–31 where he presented his case in extreme terms. In his closing arguments, Job remembered how good his life was (Job 29) and how unbearable it had become (Job 30). Finally, in an attempt to force a response from God, Job unleashed a series of oaths, calling down judgment on himself if he had not lived an innocent life (Job 31).

Remembering the Good Old Days

Job 29

Question 3: Read Job 29. List the good deeds Job was known for back when he enjoyed "the friendship of God" (Job 29:4).

_____

_____

_____

From Cause to Culprit

Job 30

Question 4: Read Job 30. List the actions Job believed God had taken against him.

_____

_____

_____

Forcing the Issue

Job 31

The Two-Part Formula of Job's Oaths in Chapter 31:
- **Part 1: If I have sinned…**
  For example, "If I have walked with falsehood…" (Job 31:8).
- **Part 2: then let disaster strike me.**
  For example, "…then let me sow, and another eat" (Job 31:8).

Question 5: Read Job 31. List or summarize the sins Job claimed to be innocent of.

_____

_____

_____

HANDOUT FOR SESSION 9

Elihu Steps In

Key Passage: Job 32–37

Passage Summary: After Job tried to force God to speak, the newcomer Elihu offered more speeches, shifting attention to God's goodness.

Main Point: Life requires patience because our words and actions cannot coerce God to speak or act.

Opening Discussion

Question 1: Tell about a time you were so thirsty that water tasted amazing.

_____

_____

_____

Question 2: Tell about a time you had to wait for God.

_____

_____

_____

Introducing...Elihu?

Job 32

We've read 29 chapters of speeches from Job and his friends. When we finally arrive at the end of Job's words, the book takes a surprising turn. Instead of a response from God, Job got four speeches from Elihu, a man we never met before chapter 32, a man who is never listed among Job's friends.

> Job must have been disappointed to hear the voice of another human being, but Elihu's appearance spoke volumes. Job learned what sovereignty means. God cannot be coerced, ever. Job's drastic measures secured none of his demands: he had wanted Yahweh; he got Elihu! WLMTS, p. 158

Question 3: Read Job 32. What motivated Elihu to speak up?

_____

_____

_____

Let's Hear Him Out

Job 33–37

Question 4: Read Job 33–34. How did Elihu summarize Job's words? If time allows, also read Job 35–37.

_____

_____

_____

Giving Elihu a Chance

> Most Old Testament scholars have not been kind to Elihu.... According to them, Elihu talked big (impetuous) but failed to deliver.... Even though Elihu talked a lot, he did not add anything to the discussion (unoriginal). After he finally finished, no one responded positively or negatively (ineffectual). WLMTS, pp. 155-56

Question 5: Look again at Job 33:23–30. Which phrases in this section remind you of your own experience with Christ?

_____

_____

_____

HANDOUT FOR SESSION 10

God Answers Job

> **Key Passage:** Job 38–42
>
> **Passage Summary:** When God finally answered Job, Job repented. God then rebuked Job's friends and restored Job.
>
> **Main Point:** A relationship with God makes it possible to worship Him, even when He doesn't answer all our questions.

Opening Discussion

Question 1: What is your favorite comeback story?

_____

_____

_____

Question 2: Tell about a time God answered you in a way you didn't expect.

_____

_____

_____

God Answers Job Out of the Whirlwind

Job 38–41

> Who is this that darkens counsel
>   by words without knowledge?
> Dress for action like a man;
>   I will question you, and you make it known to me.
> Where were you when I laid the foundation of the earth?
>   Tell me, if you have understanding. (Job 38:2–4)

> Will you even put me in the wrong?
> Will you condemn me that you may be in the right? (Job 40:8)

Question 3: Read Job 38 and 40. List the types of questions and challenges God confronted Job with. If time allows, also read Job 39 and 41.

_____

_____

_____

Question 4: How was God's response different from the response Job expected?

_____

_____

_____

Job Retracts His Lawsuit and God Restores Job

Job 42:1–17

God rebuked Eliphaz, Bildad, and Zophar saying, "You have not spoken of me what is right as my servant Job has" (Job 42:7). He commanded them to take seven bulls and seven rams and go to Job so he could offer sacrifices and a prayer on their behalf. The three friends "did what the LORD had told them, and the LORD accepted Job's prayer" (Job 42:9).

Finally, God restored Job's fortunes. He restored Job's wealth, his family, his livestock, and his friends. The book concludes with the following summary:

> And after this Job lived 140 years, and saw his sons, and his son's sons, four generations. And Job died, an old man, and full of days. (Job 42:16–17)

Made in United States
Troutdale, OR
07/07/2023

11036060R00060